P9-EDK-992

ONDINA

John Roberts

Jake Pinello

ONDINA

A Narrative Poem

John Roberts

with illustrations by
Jake Pinello

Cloud Ridge Press

The Old Man's final sentence on skiing on page 89 derives from a comment made by Sam Hamill during a reading in Golden, Colorado, in 40077. The comment is gratefully acknowledged here in honor of the spoken word and used with permission. As paraphrased for the poem, it reads as follows:

> I wouldn't mind
> if they slid down the mountains
> on their little boards,
> if they just had the common decency
> to walk up 'em.

Special thanks to Edouard Thai for his revealing translation of the Rilke passage used here as an epigraph.

Ondina is pronounced ahn-DEE-nuh.

Library of Congress Cataloguing in Publication Data

Roberts, John, 1946-
    Ondina: a narrative poem.
    I. Pinello, Jake, 1943-   . II. Title.
PS3568.O23873O55   1985   811'.54   85-24315
ISBN 0-9615617-0-x (alk. paper)
ISBN 0-9615617-1-8 (pbk. : alk. paper)

Printed in the USA
Illustrations by Jake Pinello
Book Design by Lanie Kohler

Cloud Ridge Press
P.O. Box 926
Boulder, Colorado 80306

For Lanie

Contents

You see, I want a lot.
Perhaps I want all:
the dark of each infinite fall
and the shivering light-play of each climb up.

—Rainer Maria Rilke
Translated by Edouard Thai

Book One

The Face in the Waters

I

THE Dream descends
a staircase of slow breath,
and down
as crumbling air
it crowds like fog
into the vault of all my skull
and there betrays.
Its closeness, false
as walls and dome of ash,
dissolves
in wet unending space
like deep sea rain
when night and ocean flood
their touch
and meet at no horizon.

I embark the night companion,
she who rolls
the northless dark,
the weightless,
drifting, swelling waves
of soul-immersing dark,

11

who never takes my arm,
never counsels
but engulfs,
bids me to dissolve
and float out
molecule by molecule,
as each bright bubble
of my body's foam
darkens
with the dye she opens
in my veins,
rises with the current
that she rides behind my eyes,
then lifting one by one
from my decaying face and form,
bursts
in its starlight leap
down slopes of space.

Here, there is her changing face,
huge in wafting backdrops
and black wing cloths,
lifting, falling,
the proscenium expanding,
unfolding folds
in waves of night.

This face of darkness shines
in starlight-swirled reflections of itself—
two women, old and robed,
sitting face to face across a fire
as they intone an ancient ode
into the fringy light.

In the flickers from the fire
their hook-nosed faces glow and melt,
disappear,
then reappear as youthful beauties,
keen as hawks.
Their eyes flash blue,
gray-green,
and sparkling black.
Their lips, flushed red
and plump as berries,
quiver with their spoken tones.

One is blonde,
the other dark.
But in the wild, breeze-wafted play
of fire and night,
the shadows flash
their tangled hair by turns,
each a strobe of black and white.

Then sinuous as shedding snakes,
they part the robes,
reveal the opening
of naked fullness in the night.
By turns, they bend and curl down
to tend the fire.
One blows on coals,
the other feeds in a twig,
and in the ebb and flow of dark and light,
they sway,
blur gray,
and interchange like smoke,
then merge as one,

bright-dark and whole,
emerging new,
but old and double-knowing as the Muse,
double-knowing
how to feed or eat the fire's heart,
breathe full or suck its soul.

Then she sees me darkly
dreaming through the mirror,
turns and slowly sloughs the open robe
down off her shoulders.
Her lips part to the glint of teeth.

The shadows seize me,
cast me loose
across the tundra
and I'm running,
running in a pack of shadow dogs,
running
the way of the Wolf,
knowing
bones and storm clouds,
the broke rib
as trade with Caribou,
the chilling howl
of nightsong,
and the white-dark wait
of winter.

The Dark One waits.
She fills
the hollows
scooped by fear

in an evacuated gut,
supplies the blood
and bones
and held-breath force
of quiet,
and the power of the dark
to stare.
She waits,
a cellar door
ajar.

And deeper,
she is the waiting for a stone
dropped
down the dream vault
that echoes only inhaled passage,
no report of bottom.

The Dark One waits
as deep as unborn Old Ones.
Her patience for deliverance
spreads vast as ocean floors
and filters thin
the swelling mud of prophets.
She curves my swimming soul
against this deep horizon,
slips her current
along my pull,
drifts just beyond
the swollen lip
and swirl
and spirit-sluicing suck
of the broken circle's

slave nation whirlpool of wombs.

Spun as male from a rebel mother's womb,
played out
on one remaining spider's strand
of glistening cord,
I dangle free
in the new burning air of voices,
tones of family,
tones of earth,
and hear now how even Grandpa's raspy caw
spoke of the love and death
deep-rooted in the female land.
And that old man's rasp and love
now keep me mindful
that, like his, my own rough maleness
was borne
and birthed
with female mucous
in my eyes and ears and mouth.

Imagination frightens,
but it's lack of it that kills.
And that wrong kind of killing
had made the Old Man rail:

"You run your gotdamn asphalt
through this valley,
scrape down to bone,
starve out the elk,
and eat grease.

"Doncha know?

Them big lights
chase off the stars.
Pretty soon, you can't think."

The Dark One sees
from folds of silence.
From under my own brow
she watches
as I walk and swing forth gestures,
answer
to a vision as common as a cob,
gall my hopes,
and walk and walk and talk all out
and nicely basket my obsessions, and try
to dream deep lustre
and the North of Northern Lights,
yet plow against the wild.

Here, even I,
who mostly sleep,
still dream,
dream my tiny light,
think there's something in
the thin reflected glint
of slivered moonlight,
the slice
that wakes me through Venetian blinds.
I halt
the walking dream,
turn,
pull blanket binding smoothly
to my neck
and tighten its cool satin

beneath the rainy dark,
walk on.

The rain is lighter then.
I walk on down
the steps, downhill,
and down some sloping green
and out from under dripping misplaced elms,
and then, from Russian olive groves'
wet powder smell
I break into the open,
heels sinking
slightly sinking
back into the slope
with every questioning
across huge green,
across the wild grasses,
the open reaches toward
the prairie of my hope.

And down,
the old waters gather,
down the cold mountain.
Slow streaks swell from seeps,
and rivulets from snow,
and freshets
spraying moss rock
tumble
down,
down the cold mountain,
and weigh
the thrusts of liquid
heaving by me

in this living being
we call River.

And here the gnarly
scrub oak stretches out,
lifts into reach
of cottonwood,
member of the ancient shade,
along the banks
of water,
bending, giving, flowing
once again into the heartland
and away.

Here, the Searching One
leaned
toward secrets,
watching,
her vision drifting down
across the great phantom rolls
of green and purple shadows,
breeze rich with scents,
a creature to become
Birth
on the plains,
Animal,
in wonder
of what will make her
lead a mate
from close cover,
from the sacred hills,
and out
into the wide

lavish terror
of seasons lain in grasses.

The hawk works slowly,
circling in a dream.
A dream can sort the world out,
if you can keep the voices straight.

My old friend Billy Hitch's voice
recalls a world or two.
It was the first time we were old enough
to listen to the land
and choose among its multicolored faces.
And the voices of those worlds
still echo through the dream
and then there comes the scream,
high up, the banking wings,
and still the hawk works slowly,
downwind,
then veers
into a stoop
behind the mesa.

We'll never know.

And Billy Hitch saw
his whole life in that work,
in that hawk's dive.
He dropped the stone
he'd picked from scree
to throw into the river.
Sunlight on the wing
had taught him.

He might throw again, he said,
but never heedless
toward the spirit-glint in water;
and wouldn't go to that war.
That was it.
That day by the river,
with inviting water magic
holding back a stone,
we thought we'd trudged the quicksand.

    "Too gone," he told me.
    "That's no war.
    If you go now
    you got no choice;
    you'll just be covering ass
    while they make deals.
    Hang your balls out
    for cardsharks,
    what you think they're gonna do?"

A prying light-flick
breaks the clouds.
The hawk comes up with hair,
and, like all of us
who hunger,
will hurl down again.

And age came to Billy Hitch's eyes,
the same as those of War.
Along the derrick-punctured land,
always thumbing back north
from Denver, broke,
back to Rock Springs and roughnecking,

taking the West Slope run
to cross the Divide
and start afresh like water,
he got bottomhole
in the blood
and brain
and saw his friends lose
hands and arms to wormbite,
their loves up and gone
along with repo'd trailers,
their laughs, echoes
in the treasure tombs
of boom town honky tonk walls.

"Blowout
sends a rig up like a Christmas tree,
a dry one,
blowtorch trunk.
No shit.
People crinkle.

"And cold?
And wind?
Kuba working crown
one day,
hell, one hour
and his hands went out on him;
like trying to grab rungs
with ball bats.
Hunnert feet—
I swear he arced out
in that wind,
that wind going like *ex-spress*.

"A Jesus freak picked me up
cold day outta Kremmling
and upset me talkin,
telling me I didn't have to work.
Says he's a reverend
and he knows.
His Lord'll do it for us.
That's what he said.
He was real inspired,
and I kept ridin.
Hours of it.
And he smelled
like a guy all the time taking
hot showers.
Took me right out to the rig.
One of those days it was so cold
your mind crackled,
so cold
you could hold diesel fuel
in your hands like jelly.
And I said, *Wait*;
went and got a handful,
brought it back and dumped it
right in his lap.
Communion time.
Ruint a good pair-a
buck mitts.
Still think
that guy a little rude,
talkin Jesus
to me a total stranger.
Real reverends,
they don't say nuthin.

"Don't worry.
EXXON'll take care of everything.

"But the foxes sure like coke.
They go down for coke.
Spend all my money
on coke."

II

ANOTHER roll of clouds
tears slowly open,
low across the upthrust
ridge of weathered rock.
The April sun
comes late this year; filtered,
cantilevered squirts
of its pale lemon
spike and burst
and spray down mist-light colonnades,
cool phosphorescence through
still shaded air.

Another breath,
air full of shadows,
but now this mist commingles
in their smoke.
Its moistness tingles
on my lids as light.
Is it enough?
Enough, I say,
and lift my face

and try to push this pale gazing
into the fullest spray.
Well, then, you Dark One,
look.
Squint and rub your eyes.
Spray burns, you say?
Well, smoke burns mine.
And so we miss
a stroke
and stumble past this blank white sign,
one leg each, jerking
in the other's sack,
till back in step,
we walk into the warm
deep river of my lungs
to swell and drift,
and once again faint mist
is lost
in wetness.

One blows on coals,
the other feeds in a twig.

Come under, comes the call.
Drift down.
Breathe the fluid of your sleep
and fall to sea.
I feel its pull,
its down-compressing weight,
its invitation
to the deep and heavy looseness,
taste of woman,
plunge of lips,

the weight of thighs
compressed against my ears,
against the rush of blood,
against the pounding
dark compounding
of the name I cannot hear.
The killer and the healer in me
will not hear: Ondina—
nor hear that Karin drowned her,
drowned Ondina, drowned.
Ondina, take your eyes,
the body balm
of nights at sea.
Ondina,
take those sea-gray eyes
or see me drown in them
and in their watching,
washing over me that slides away
and echoes night surf
down the slopes of vast within.

Ondina,
this Dark Old One steals your eyes.
Take those eyes.
Keep them from her;
swear me blind
and innocent beyond
her vision of my breath and light.
They pull.
They empty,
make me tumble in my swim
and pull against
Dark Old One's pull

and press my thumbs
into the seeing Ocean's eyes.
Sucked under;
thumbs plunge knuckle deep
in dark Ondina's eyes.

Towed down,
I feel the swirl of blackest blood
flood cold the light.
Old One, lead me;
don't deny me.
Yes, I see her,
meet her eyes here, want
her whispers in my coat.

The face in the wavy mirror
says, *You've been raving.*
Look again.

Waking to the world of wetness,
he bends,
so casually sits down,
watches, sees her face
here in the water and the grass.
Here where Mountains ease
their shoulders
into the breastbone
of the Plains
and meet as one the bend
of River,
here where grasses finger
gravel banks,
he begins to see the power

as he flicks a pebble,
flick—
a pebble arcs out over moving water
till the river's hush
takes in its kissed *ku-plorp*
and whirls like a smile.

As casually as sinking,
his sitting down becomes a quest,
and he searches through the swirls
for the one who didn't die
and meets her eyes
here, *flick*—the living touch of death—
searching,
even as he's flicking pebbles
in her breath.

Book Two

Record of Small Matters
in Dress of Mourning

I

He lounges akimbo on the grass,
looking toward the river
from the hillcrest where his house sits,
then down at blades of grass
between his legs.

Rapt in thanks
or fights,
through gnarls of despair
or searching prayer,
or disengaged toward vision,
the eye must level,
float on free,
expanding curve and balance
from its place.

He heard the Old Man say,
    "The bowed head
    aint no way
    to meditate—
    or bite."

But he forgets.
The crookt spine
recurves an openness,
and some chance
of Universe
slips him a blow
behind his back.

Among the storm's last raindrops,
one falls, *ptack*,
upon bare nape,
piercing
as good clean acid cutting deep
in shivers,
and he feels the froth of scouring
float
up
and out of him
across the surface
of the sky;
and he knows something has passed,
looks up
and sees it broken, drifting
in trails
of broken clouds
like foam
in tidal pools.

Her face rises, looms
through damp air caught staring,
through evaporation, haze,
and streaks of clouds.

But he mistook
the lights in those blue-gray eyes.
Contact melted them to shadow gray
like snow bowls
touched by sun.
He saw their offerings melt away
like dusk or dawn, the twilight power of tears,
aspiring to the troughs
of winter seas,
but missed the flowing hook-beaked beauty
at her leisure beneath the sorrow
of a gull wing
dipped to a wave.

For as such troughs
pull back beneath the waves,
the surfaces, the liquid flow
of graying eyes
sucked back still darker
till her eyes had no surfaces at all,
no more than whirlpools
have surfaces, beyond enchantment.

Deep in whirling turns,
he fell in mortal fascination
of his fear,
feeling secrets
sucked from him and drowned,
washed north and frozen—
dead, embraced and dead
before they ever told themselves to him.

But the untold

brings him all the same
to peer,
to see just
over
the lip edge,
a cauldron,
a roiling name aberrant born
of Earth
and Sea,
a primal fright: Charybdis.
And he liked it,
rank and murderous as it sounded.
He swayed within its vapor,
stirred it thickly with his hand,
scooping
the emulsion of his fears to taste.

And these grassy banks
and lowlands
fell under wheels first.
The eye's horizon
stretched no more,
and he lost the vision,
the rolling moans,
the *montes veneris mons*
of the long grasses
to flat lawns and blinking groves,
aching new in the sun.
And the word for world
was *clipped*.

But nape hairs,
vestigial sensors

of surprise
and thrill of dark,
the slash of fear
and Old Awareness that meant Life,
still fringe
the dorsal
being
with connections to the vibrant
thing that waits
to seethe
and boil up living,
bearing power
of ancient pulse
to shoots and bud tips,
greening cracks
in concrete,
pollen,
blowing wild
from unsurrendered swales
and corner brambles
missed by mowers.

The cocoon splits
along its back.
The first wet shivers
are of wings.

II

FROM across the new short cut grass,
where they've sodded out a stand of prairie
for a park,
he looks toward the old house of bricks
with its rascally fringe of bluestem
and sees the rooted battle lines for time.

And the Dark Four-legged One
runs off through silence
into song.
Still, from across the dark
bare ice,
from the rhythm
of the run,
still comes the song,
song of swaying,
song of moving on,
the song of footprints
melting in the snow:

> Crumbling home made of ice
> Fluid home made of waves;

Crumbling home made of earth
Fluid home made of quakes;

Crumbling home made of stone
Fluid home made of hums;

Crumbling home made of logs
Fluid home made of flame;

Crumbling home made of hands
Fluid home made of light;

Crumbling home made of breath
Fluid home made of night;

Crumbling home made of blood
Fluid crumbling made of home;

Crumbling fluid running home
Fluid calling, calling home:

How long home?
How long crumbling?
How long are,
Long uncrumbling,
Fluid bodies in the tar?

And he could smell the fixer
from the photograph
the doctors had given him.
In it, her eyes
had changed.

He knew then, even as Charybdis
could not whirl down and in forever,
so must Ondina's eyes
boil back up now,
spattering shadows
through these grasslets sprouting
out of winterkill.

Yet within the surging
there is stillness,
and the afternoon's rain,
fallen,
spreading now like dew
in the second morning of the day,
touches
through his trousers
and the elbows of his coat.
He shifts upright,
soaked in aches
so clean and late.

Now cross-legged on the grass,
he reaches out,
pinches
a single blade,
draws it slowly through
its sheath of tatters,
baring its new season full
of secrets.

The blade's load of winter
presses grit
against his thumb and finger.

That, he thinks, is nothing.
He wants the white end,
glistening,
just beginning to lean
toward green.
He places it between
the edges
of two front teeth
and bites
four times.

Inside his head, he hears
the sounds of yielding.
Cell crusts give,
giving as raw
hides of Caribou
chewed
pliable
by women,
all their teeth nubbed
down, for him.

His mind spans
the eurythmics
of a moccasin in snow.
Juices spatter
on his palate,
then disappear
into the wetness of his mouth.

And he thinks: No, these cameo
intrusions of Ondina's eyes
are wrong.

This is the taste of dreams
and nothing else.

He snap-turns his head
to catch the encroaching
ambush of the grass,
sends the shadows scattering back
under he groves,
on over the hillcrest,
and down the cobbled
banks of the river,
holds them there with his gaze, looks
across from bank to bank for confirmation.

Into focus comes
an atom of black gnats,
arcing
silver circles through slants of sun.
Flits of shade.

And in the quiet
there was K, dream woman
of the North.
Sometimes Karin, sometimes Kate,
she turned the seasons of his fantasies,
the measure of ideal,
and dared now wield
the power of magnetic north, askew
in the true presence
of Ondina's shadowed ken.

He thinks of how this conjured
woman's laugh comports

within the stillness held
between Ondina's breasts.
How crazy blind K made him;
how he had never known
she worked against him;
how she had not known either;
and how the difference
was known only to the grass.

A winter's guest
was how he advertized
for the apartment in the basement,
and his mind constructed Karin,
who would come alone to sign.
Her voice of early mammal
would come in low,
in through his gut,
the tones,
I am Ondina,
coming as plain-faced
surprise
from under Kate.
And she had legs and legs and legs;
her hips,
strong and dolphin fluent,
would give
to movement easy
as a dancer, bathing
after a performance,
strut gone,
perfumed of sweat
and promise.

This cassolette of reverie
infused
the plain milk scent
Ondina stood in at his door.
And the K
he imposed on her
would be the flare above the shade
that dazed
when, much later,
he got close enough
for that first taste of amber bitters
behind a lobe.

Of course, the new paint pleased her,
seashell white against the oaken
woodwork rubbed by hand.
And of the basement
she said, *I like wintering
underground.*

Those were the barely breathing
weeks of January,
which died in freeze
and slid on
into storage locker skies
of February, held in windless cold.

But he had bestowed the dream,
and there was K,
draped
about this creature,
warm enough,
he thought. He reached

45

to warm his hands under
this mantle,
felt the shoulders of Ondina.
Yes, warm enough;
and he watched those legs ridge
up under layered dresses,
slow rearing,
arched back guiding,
breath, insistent throb—
then light,
shattering!
Her eyes?
No, Karin's.
Whose?
K's or O's?
And he knew the sun caught ice.
As winter, this spring nymph
would sharpen tricks
each year on someone new,
cause him to believe
he could make it through
the dark
and cold
without something in him dying.

Still, he got wet over her
but saw then, instead of gray,
sharp blue-green berylline
of eyes;
and when her hair fell,
brown and loose,
he described the fair red-gold it caught
from a paper globe around the lamp

and nudged himself just through the opening
of vision in her mammal song of moans.

Disembodied as the dream
was this dark witness to it all,
this bystander,
this Other to Dark Old One.
She gave him tea,
light-dark swirlings in a cup.
He felt the full brew
of herbal tastes
slide into him,
the stone lip
giving fluid,
and he swallowed
the rooted dangers
earth holds deep
for the unknowing
but would not know
that it was she, hair wild,
who was in him,
Ondina,
toothed and seasonal and naked, turning,
Ondina,
the dark youngling
of the Old.

III

ONDINA took up lodging in his mind
as concierge to longing,
the shadow greeting
in the cave of true sleep
or delusion,
the wonder
and the woe
of two women come acknowledged
in the muffled stirrings
beneath his floors.

He remembered now
how time swirls
and eddies back.
It had been once when he swung
on the basement door,
a whim,
a half-hop half-swoop down
on the hinged carousel
to clear the four steps to the landing
between
upstairs and down,

but bumped,
stumbled.
Ondina and a basket stuffed with laundry
shoved hard against the wall.
Her head banged,
and he felt a wedge of heel slip
the top step and start to tip
him
full-length down the stairs.
His cheekbone scribed an arc, uncrushed,
just brushed
her lip,
wet edge of teeth.
He saw wide darkness down her mouth,
felt his eye dry
in her throat's quick suck of air.
The basket dumped
as they first touched, jostled,
knee-deep in towels and underwear.
Entangled and free,
losing to the ledge,
he knew again forever
the weightless instant
off the sheer-wall
of the Diamond
before he took the ripper
of the rope,
the lifting *Whump* and body-toss
of a mortar in the mud,
and the soft rush
of desert air
as the mare
tripped

and heaved downslope
toward the canyon cut;
then he felt Ondina's palm
catch full
of hip and pull
tight an arm around his waist.

Stairwell agape.
The moment
still expands.

Regained, they stood face to face.
He heard some far off calling come
through the pounding quiet
from across the loosened hold.

They bent to pick things up,
bumped heads, and he flashed
on being expelled from Dance,
knew they would be marked
by syncopation, clog shoes,
and miscalculated closeness.
He forgave himself for wanting
Karin's laugh
as buffer,
this distant silence
caving in his ears.
Then thought it funny.

Ondina did not smile,
and he heard his voice start, fall
out of cadence,
still itself.

He saw some black piece—
a chess knight?—swing
from a silver chain around her neck.
It jerked and bobbed
against her breasts
as she dipped in
and out
of the basket.
Its head peeked
from the V
of her blouse, loose gauze.
She was bare
white underneath;
her throat plunged
down fragile shadow edges
and winged out into collar bones
that spread gliding like an egret.

A green wool cape
draped about her shoulders,
but still, he thought,
she'll freeze.
Breath will cloud
and stuff her lungs with snow.

Lowered eyes
now masked her face,
androgynous as clay.
And though her breasts held radiance,
fluffed out white
against the cold like plumage,
he shuddered seeing them so open
there in the draft

with that black horse,
which tumbled out then as she bent,
threatened knight fork
to distract him. Still
not one at that time to avert
his eyes,
he glimpsed a nipple's
knurled pink.

But it was the knight
which had first brought the look.
And it was that vision,
the first sighting of the horse's head,
which now became deep-dyed
across the night screen
of his eyelids.

As in the mirrored
image of himself
when sliding a necktie, cool
beneath his collar,
her knight made its connection
slowly,
backhand over hand.

That tie.
He had had it on,
its silver silk
the color of her chain,
and it, too, had held a black knight,
Bangkok embroidered handwork,
Staunton rendered
unfamiliar

in Asian curls.
He believed spirits waited
in the pattern,
shifted
for the knowing
into nostrils
and wide stare of horsehead.

Then a fastener had snagged the tie.
This creature
had continued silent,
had helped him get untangled.
Would she see it,
talk about
why both of them had chess knights
round their necks?
Familiar ground.

He would tell
about his having won the tie
as veteran of clock strategy
and college tours,
a combat grunt let out to prey
on student monks—
maybe leaving out
the part on poor attendance,
and how that had been his last:
He had set a jungle
on the board.
The guy had lost his head.
Chess fooled
the T-square mind
seduced by angles.

The side-pounce tracks
of the mountain cat
are not noted in the texts,
of which study gives pursuit
but, lacking alchemy,
can let the stars
all spin away.

But what if he were just inflamed?
How could he explain, unless
she saw the spirits move the tie?
The knight gave something real
after
first not being
there at all.

Ondina did not ask.

Nice horse, he said.

Ondina took a breath
and looked away.
She bent again to knead
the clothes down deeper in the basket.
He thought he caught
the scent
of night-grown yeast
rising warmly from the huge white
dough of sheet
pushed out amongst her fingers.
But no, not then. Not yet.
Last night was dreamed.

Play much?
he asked as he looked down at her.

She brought a late hand
to her throat.
A frown
then might have touched her face.
She stood.
Expression vanished,
smoothed away
in plain wet clay.
And the knight, too, had dropped back
into hiding,
just its head above the cloth.

He stooped for the basket,
raised up,
and held it out for her.
She took it,
and the knight pressed
its wooden ears into the fastness,
disappeared
behind breast-clamped wads of clothes.

Now cool grass rises all around,
but the knight's sinking
back among her secrets
is what lays the cold hand
on his chest.
Yes, he sees it,
now can feel it,
thinks it real enough,
a roughly assembled fate charm,

makeshift,
though as deliberate
as quick.

The silver chain was finely linked,
a lanyard, fluid
as thick silk, which looped
around the horse's neck,
fixed simply with a knot
beneath its chin.

The knight hung
crookedly,
its head atilt,
its nose cocked
up
in either a gasp or a snort.

Someone else
might have drilled a tiny hole
or screwed an eyelet
in the mane
to let the chain
pass through
and display the piece attractively.
Of course, he thinks, such late
pointing shadows
do not matter to the grass.
Grass knows its course.

He sees himself again,
holding the door
for her, wrong side,

making a high archway
with one arm.
She'd ducked through it, stepped
easily outside
and down the back porch steps,
merging with black-bright
evening ink
along the glazed back walk.
Nice move, he'd thought,
for a plain woman
with a load of wash.

Now the wince
indicts,
and he knows he missed
the shadow of clear grace.
Even now he searches.

Sometimes his eye snags
stray movements.
Peripheries
tug him out of other moments,
and he sees
Ondina's small back, fading
in the black and silver
of a winter night,
down the lane
to feed the roan
or check the mailbox,
her hair swept up,
snow reflections
lambent on her nape
in wisps.

Or she appears along the road,
quarter-sideways walking,
one shoulder slung
with her brown pack strap,
arm out low
to hitch a pickup,
left heel arcing last
beyond the neighbor's yard light.

Other times it's someone watching him.
A curve of face
becomes a bole
of willow,
a roll of river,
sun-pillowed water
over stone,
a shoulder
stretch,
refolding wing
of Owl.

Or he sees her coming toward him,
emerging
from the hedge shadows
and walking toward him
across the crusty snowed-down grass,
staring,
emptying him with those eyes.
And in walking toward him,
she knows.
And on
still toward him—
He tries to speak.

And closer,
he feels her probe his fear,
measure breaths
like stairs
to take or fall upon.
Then right close in,
she looks away,
and worse, what he fears most:
In his dream to scent her hair,
she pities him.

Then it breaks between them,
artificial as a vacuum seal,
the force of held breath,
collapsing
as it's freed.
So sucked behind retreating eyes,
the power is gone
before it gathers into speech.
They pass,
offer a nod.
He feels the urge to wave,
as if from a canoe across the lake.

He endures these gestures
as he endures
the nuisance of wiping bath vapor
off a mirror;
he never sees her, sees
his own reflection
stopped
in some blank act.

Then there is his desire
staring back.
Ondina disappears
into the crowding fog
but leaves her cloak
unguarded
in his hand,
and Karin figures
from the mist,
hands on hips.
He sees her step
from shadows, dim,
then quietly descend
the stairs,
down, back down the spiral stairs
on silken-stockinged feet.
Believe,
she says, *Believe,*
tosses hair,
and motions for the cloak.

This K rewards
wakeful unwakening,
the night courage
to follow dreams,
braving conversation, faced
with O's wet-cavern quiet.
But in life-giving danger—
the heart of stillness
of his dream—
Ondina's stairway, leading
down into the basement,
keeps plunging deeper.

Giving lie
to the bravery of a staircase,
he descends
with trepidation,
turns up lights,
pretends
to talk with O
as he conjures up his Kate,
denying either knows
he could not meet
those eyes—
dusk graying to night blue, leading toward
rich dark—
but through the amber air of fraud.

Mostly, though, the rooms were bright,
webbed
ceilings gauzed
with captured light.

The walls were warmed by tapestries
and lithographs,
all Karin's, he presumed;
and the necessary pipes,
although not masked,
were blended well enough
and served for hanging ferns
and ivies
and planter boxes
ragged
with hyssop and blue cohosh,
unpinched basil,
fuzzy winter marjoram,

hair-clump chives,
and chervil,
wizard thyme,
Joe-Pye weed,
calendula,
and other dark-leafed herbs
and sprouts of sharp
unbounded scents.
They grew strong
and hairy
in flats and baskets slung
before a surprising lot
of garden-level windows for a basement.

Still, the rooms
once quartered servants;
and crowded turns
and niches
pitted dusk
against the comfort
of those who worked and lived
for others,
harbored angst
of cells,
and gave at random
unto coal bin alcoves,
halls and doorways
inhabited
by something larger than the light.
Down into these,
the night
stairs
led either their apprentice

or their prey.

He loathed
when Karin was not ready.
O would show him in
then turn to dough,
unleavened
in a ritual aloof
from bursting yeast.
And in her voice
he heard the mollifying puff
of handmaiden,
explaining
to the gentleman,
The Lady
is not in this evening.
Take chamomile tea?

Yet he ached
to mold resilience
in his hands,
came to her in sudden
guileless want.
She opened her dress
and took him close
and deep
without the cloak
and rolled him full sway in Female,
the huge pull of waves of dark,
the drowning, soothing, terrifying floods
of secrets,
unknowable within the rush
of cries

from out her grace.

But uncaged,
no more pacing at the bars,
no longer captive of composure,
nor of cool fingers
on his nape,
he stalked her fear-wet scent
and slid down past her eyes,
felt the tear and terror
seize him in her hands' seizing
fists of hair,
as he sank teeth
into her thigh
and into woman-folds
and drank.

Book Three

The Bitch Root

I

HE marvelled how enchantment draped
the dying.
Except for her small talisman
of black and silver,
he thought the cloaking near complete;
though still, he sensed
she held the power
in the quiet
waiting, knowing of her knight
to draw him under
with those eyes
and slip the hood.

Thinking? Or dreaming? she asked,
eyes pulling, wholly gray of O.

I really haven't time these days,
he said, *for games.*

Like chess? she asked.
A teasing smile.

He: *No, not chess. Why do you wear—?*
He gestured to the knight.

She: *Yes, well. Chess does take time.*

Too much, he said.
Perhaps I'll have more time
to play
when I get old.
Held out the cape.

Maybe Chess, she said,
is someone who'd be pleased
to grow old with you.

And the out-tide
eyes
of Woman-sea
withdrew from searching at the cliff,
slid down the beach
and left the garments
of the drowned.

He felt he only shifted, held
against the tide
and knew as sand and shore
a tidal pull
was force diminished
by retreat.
Ondina's ocean swelled
with the pallor of the moon;
while his bright sorcery,
he thought,

70

drew blood.

Sanguine Karin soon became quite busy
with her pic,
first mulching
easy pasture
then prodding
him, hoof pawing,
out of it toward earthier
arenas of her own.

At first he choked
with charge and halt,
and she kept it up
and kept it up,
as if her touch
could both set off
and still hold back
exploding pain.

And pass after pass,
he hooked moist air,
flank shivers brushing by,
and she wound him around her
in great swinging,
circling veronicas,
and then, without melting,
those lips said soft
Goodnight,
and she left him, fixed
and dazed,
to watch her cape
float

down those awful stairs,
and not to see her flashing blade
till later,
when alone in his room,
from his jacket
pocket,
a note which read:
    Tired
    of finding stairway door locked.
    Afraid you'll be discovered
    in your drop-seat pajamas?

With desire guised as Fate,
he could convince himself she loved him
by her sudden piercings,
the melt, thick
as blood down his sides,
by all the times
that winter when heat
had mocked the snow,
and by the voice,
    Believe, believe,
he heard from wine and wind
and once steaming
and entangled beneath
the spring-dark
magic of her cape
in the deserted, sifting cold
along the river bank.

Then came the night he knew.
The stairs knew,
and the plants knew,

and the eyes.

Waiting, perched
on quilted floor cushions,
he felt himself float out
and drift into the quiet,
the denied presence of liquid space
between
one breath out
and one breath in.

Where was K's exhaled laugh?

He saw a spider
watching
from its crack.

It was a rivalry for silence,
for dominion.
The soft surrounds
of fear pushed
its pillows to his face.
No, he thought, the air
is always thicker in a basement.
He challenged it aloud, *Silence,*
and huffed a laugh.

The quiet broke within its name
but did not break the change
which now pulled down
on him in black surprise
of undertow.

Fathoms flooded fathoms,
backflushing warmth
for chills.
He felt the thermal turnover
of lakes.
Shadows swelled his vision,
rose from underneath, a river
rising in the night
to wash
the moonbright fields of youth
where he had splashed
in knee-deep floods
and splattered floating melons
with a kick,
enough to end as silt
packed in a shoe.

He heard his voice cry out
above the slow
dark soak
of river-rise,
cry out alone
against the stillness
and felt the swirl
of quiet's first down-sucking current
heave toward the gulf
of seasoned seas.
He feared beneath his voice
the women only gathered strength, waited
in undertows of silence
for him to sleep.

He called out louder,

holding back the scream,
Silence!?
trying to intone warning,
but he heard from deep in marrow
the sound of stone ax
on bone,
felt in the crunching chill
a beckoning.

In calling, he was called.
And before he regained breath
to voice protection,
he saw a woman's face
in wonder
of scraped flesh beneath her nails.

Quiet as a seed bed,
Ondina stared
from limbo in the forest hall.
Eyes, whirled gray of killing blue,
beyond brood flecks of green,
came
toward him;
then she passed into the kitchen,
lit the stove.

She crumbled cinnamon
and stirred hot chocolate,
served it with a dice of yarrow
and blackberry leaves,
a red seed cascade of sumac,
a burnt-umber stretch of wild honey,
and one frost-blue berry ball

from juniper
crushed
into the whole earth brew
of molten cocoa—
not a word,
her unheard breath
the even theme
beneath the clink of spoons
and the rubato
of liquid gurgling
up the sides of mugs,
her hidden eyes still watching
from poured swirls.

In the steam
he smelt
the fertile, potent
herbal oils
and humus foam
of lathered earth—
Karin?
stepping from the bath?
Then liquid dark,
so suddenly delicious,
passed his lips;
and some slippery liquid
caress of vision—
Ondina of the Plains,
true Ondina,
O of Ocean,
O of Grass—
touched him on the breastbone,
beckoned, led him,

walking down,
down the slope,
down the cold mountain,
coming home to the winds,
to the rich vision at the fringe
of the open country
where the sun stretched
and he could see
Life's fullest flow of Death
easing out across the land,
coming, coming,
surrounding, always coming
bright as breeze waves
through the grass;
where in the beauty
of their hands
all came to them
as they opened flesh
with teeth and sucked
the dark sweet meat;
where wet flows
of Woman
pulled him deep
into her belly,
and the swelling
navel
held the earth;
where she rolled
the crisp spikelets
between her hands
and held the kernels
out to him,
the glume chaff

twirling wild in the wind,
lifting
away like butterflies
wafting in their final dance.

But he struggled,
swam, and faltered
in the moils of steam.
The Black Four-legged One,
Grandfather Dog, passed him by,
headed down the draw
in an even stot,
dipped once
behind the hillock
and away.
And the taste
stayed in the crumbling house
where he awoke
to hear her say:
All the names
you call out in the night
begin with K.
I see them capitalized:
Karom, Kari, Kara, Kay,
Kenai, Kanight—
     hidden,
     hidden night hidden
     in a side-pounce move—
like piece names
in chess books.

The night smile
caught him in its curve,

and skim of cocoa
puckered
in his cup.

He rose to say goodnight.
She reached out
her hand—hesitated—
then put a finger
to her lips.

From far away,
there came the barks of dogs.

Quickly, he took the loden hooded cloak
alone
and tried to leave,
but climbing up, felt eyes
like hoarfrost
on his back.
He would stiffen on the stairs
this way and freeze.

So he stepped down,
down;
he stepped
back down,
walked past her
through the darkened hallway
to her room,
took his shirts and jackets
and a robe,
shouldered the cloak,
and left.

II

Outside,
ice spread in splinters
down the walk
and webbed out beyond
in starlit crystal lacings
through the woods
and crackled underfoot.
Hear that? asked Karin,
from the temper
of her one last try
beneath the cloak.
When ice won't melt,
it cracks.

III

TIME'S commingled spiral
turns the blackness
and the light
within the pupil
of its own tail-feeding coil.

He knew the quick and slow
edgeless blur
of turning seasons;
but for one who holds
a frozen moment,
the warming tilt begins
to foul.

Late March reeked thaw,
and then by April
he'd sniffed the shame,
unrotting stench,
and he longed for earth's sweet stink
in its rank cleansing of the compost.
But from beneath his floors
dismissal

issued up like gas.
She was coolly *yes* to music,
yes to friends,
yes, but aloof, when met on river walks,
even *yes,* with a shrug, to some forgiving,
but rue and *no*
to renewed trust;
although the sky's thin membrane
had begun to seep its gray,
and longer days swelled,
threatened to break blue
with every morning.
And he remembered:
Those who play too cautious chess
only look good losing.

So he quit the wait,
packed old-friend boots,
long nicked Nordics,
and drove west,
then climbed to sun.

He hoped
he might still find some powder
from late, high-country blows
left swirling down the north slopes—
white whirlpools—
to reach cross-country
in the snowlands
and get lost in,
deep
in the high lonely bowls
where all things of surprise

stay possible.

Then breaking
out of night
along the highbeam
forest curves of highway,
he sees ahead
the blue and red
flashers.

He rolls by in a slow
lone-man cortege.
Troopers cleaning up
a head-on.
One dead.
Passing in slow silence,
he sees a covered stretcher,
a woman's boots
sticking out at the dawn.

The turnoff just beyond
lay drifted
beneath collapsing hollow crusts,
melt tunnels for the dead.
And he found the boulder
sloughing snow
from pink quartz and granite shoulders
and the butt end
of the fir log
where the purple penstemon
would poke out
come high-country spring.

Trusting to the forest,
he struck
up the old road,
tranny whining,
wheels slipping,
bucking out of place.
Snow and Mud-melt
don't care for ruts.
And he slithered on,
urged on toward
the final slow
fish-tailed surgings
in exhausted, spawn-run gulps,
scooped shoals of white
till Winter-Spring bulged
snow muscle
against the unfit grillwork
and bogged the truck.

Clamp on skis
in the white quiet.
Say low incantations
over knees
and push up the hill,
uphill, sacred passage,
trudge-glide-trudge.

Coyote crosses wind sweep,
loping easy,
stops to give a look
and offers the sounds of breath
from under gray-mist winter aspen limbs
and on up into the quiet

blue stretch
of spruce and fir,
apparition of Grandfather Dog,
breathing,
Kai-YO-té
Cah-YO-té
Co
    YO
       té
and gone.

Sun hits.
Things get a little wet;
low meadows, waking in the dappled
warm-cold waves
of clearing off,
gurgle under melt.
And he finds in moving water sounds
the place to stay,
to eat,
to live.

Blue-green needles, frosted white,
blue-white
against the sparkle pricks
of water drips.
Melt music.
Eagle.
Raven.
Yellow Marmot, gone,
left tracks to the wind
and a sunken hole,
half dug out,

then burrowed back to sleep.
Mountain Bluebird,
male, female.
Chickadee flits her shadow
into bright white strike
of sun on snow
and he sees Ondina
and he knows
he must bring himself
yet deeper into the living country,
let loose a fitting song
and sing it back into the quiet deeps of O,
learning from the woman
the moons of how to live real blood
and, looking,
casting out across the meadowed basin
into the needle-woven valleys
and down along the ponderosa fringes
toward the plains,
hunt
and work
and be.

And the Old Man had told him so,
gnarled finger pointing
out across the land:
    "Don't get away
    for recreation;
    get away *from* it.
    That aint life,
    aint even fun.
    You start with two hints out here:
    horsehide gloves in summer,

buckskin gloves in winter.
The rest you learn
from your own touch on the ground;
from a friend here and there;
from your father, strong or wrecked;
from your mother, weaver or witch;
from a woman, if you're big enough;
from sons and daughters, eating you out
    and giving back heartache and laughs;
from the way a cougar works the edges
    and a caddis fly comes up;
from the world in the eye of a wet-titted elk
    as she dies for your meat;
from seeing something in snow
besides a skid row
for snots.
You know—?
I wouldn't mind
if they slid down the mountains
on their little boards,
if they just had the common decency
to walk up 'em."

So walk and walk
the way he says.
That part is right.
Walk the way.
Each night and day.
Move and stand,
listen,
play,
scout, feel,
feel out the land

for home.
Every day.
Stand by it
with the water,
with the weather,
with the creatures,
with the ground.
Break your back
and freeze.
You'll learn the ways
of real ease
and end up strong enough to fly.
Look.
Find the clearing.
Here,
make the home
where home is made.
Come home.
    Come home of light.
    Come home of flame.
    Come home of ice,
            of stone,
            of hums.
    Come home of earth.
    Come home of waves.
    Come home of wilds,
            of blood,
            of quakes.
    Come home of paws.
    Come home of hands.
    Come home of clan,
            of dance,
            of dream.

Come home of womb.
Come home of death.
Come home of song,
        night swirl
        of breath.
Come home.
    Come home.
    Come on,
        come home.

Sun chutes.
Shade.
Quiet.
Wool-shirt warm,
then just bare shoulders
to the wonder of the cold.
Heat waves from snow.
Wind-cut snow sculpts
a turn of hip;
a palm-cupped vulva;
a she-wolf eats the sun, the moon,
and births
another world
beneath the liquid stars
and other shapes one-season rare—
with wind, one night,
one roll
of breath, recurved.

Creek laced with ice,
serrated teeth, blade-sharp,
glint along the edges, exposed
in holes

through billowed snow.
Melt music,
water starting home
again, across the continent.
Wind sweeps snow smoke
off the peaks.
And every day
he started back late,
then stayed.
The snow cave, high upslope
from where their house would stand,
sagged just before each nightfall,
then iced over.

"You could make it here,
but not alone, not alone
and make it good, I mean.
But work the beetle-killt pine below,
and up there, the standing dead.
Lotsa good spruce
standing dead.
Just don't forget:
leave some for Flicker
and them Black Downies—
sumbitchin headknockers'll
show you how to work.

"Don't be runnin away, now.
We're spread out but it's community,
and there's worlds to do.
First year, get set up right:
Walk the winds.
Janitor a day or two a week down to the school,

just till you get it goin.
Pitch in with Sama Killdeer on her computer;
those kids are gettin sun juice
and know music
and medicine—birdwings and spaceshots.
Help Jerry with the greenhouse.
Jan'll do your truck
and trade you parts and tools.
Get them fool beeves
off that slope down there where the grass
wants to go crazy.
Sell 'em off come fall.
For God's sake,
don't eat the suckers.
Let the elk come back.
Make your trust with them.
Grass'll grow up to the belly
of your horse.
Crazy—
the kind of crazy keeps
your water clean.

"Pick up what you can.
Mind the sun,
and quit burnin everything.
Study up and cogitate.
Aint so hard's you think.
The whole thing's a-comin round.
Meantime, let the cold
scare hell outta you;
makes a lotta room
for a soul.
You could make it all along here,

make it good,
you and a woman
knows the plants."

Then down,
skiing down the frozen trail,
down the cold mountain,
down,
trying to catch
the edge of shadow
going down,
sunlight slanting just ahead,
then fading,
ice grinding ski bottoms,
hard falls,
heading back into the dusk,
scrambling through late hopes.
    She'll come.
    She'll come.

Then arcing through a curve,
arcing out like Kuba off the rig crown,
like a pebble flicked toward river whorls,
he felt the raspy ice
catch a ski
and saw the rushing tree,
the exploding wildflower *flash.*
He was flying!
Streaking!
He was Comet,
smearing icy fire
like blood through trackless dark.
And when it all fell dark, he saw the women

bending over him,
one to feed or eat the fire's heart,
the other to breathe full or suck its soul.

And all along the slope,
the blue-green boughs
touched next the passage
of the ones before, brushed
live needle fingers
against stark wood
popped spiral
yellow, whiting out,
bark gone,
wetness drained
as winter-bitten grass.
And to the grass, new tips,
new ends pumped full
of ancient waters
from the ending flow
of ending spruce,
standing down the cold mountain,
standing in the living tangle,
standing dead.

IV

THE river braids of Dream
bore his mind toward home,
spinning him through eddies of unguarded change.
He thought he would slow down a moment, wait
for the late-rising moon
to open up the night.
He saw the days had gathered sun.
The last gray crusts of snow
along the north side of the house
had disappeared.
The ground shone,
rich
as deep Dutch chocolate
in the moonlight.
The dark basement windows,
streaked with runoff,
gleamed.

With the morning came the message;
the ride to headquarters
carried him as loose as silt
where the river glides into the plains' old sea.

Then drifting toward him,
a sea horse toward the glass,
the photograph—
Ondina.

That's through the furnace room window
from outside, said the officer in charge.
Like roots, the branching pipes
tangled in his mind.
The place smelled of hospital.
A dark uniform flashed white.
He saw someone bend down and peer into a gauge
and thought he heard the officer continue,
The meter man first saw her
when he leaned down to take his reading.

Fissured, the tide gate drained
the pool's light.
He fought a pulling purple
and the yaw
of liquid dark.
Then whirling in a gurge,
he felt Charybdis
suck down on him
and felt himself go
under
and away with her,
swallowed smooth
in waves of peristalsis,
falling deeper, swallowed
with the ocean of her soul,
drifting, turning,
slowly down,

committing
softly to slow vertigo.

    Now in the grass
    he sees again
    the file photo of Spring-melt,
    her head cocked slightly,
    jawline thrust,
    her face uplifted and half turned
    toward window light,
    trying to peek out through
    one pane,
    pegging a glance
    that might precede wry curves,
    almost a smile.
    And her eyes,
    so blue-green wide
    and gray and beautiful and frozen
    in
    and out
    of rhythm.

Impossibly far off, a voice.
The officer,
now asking him to put within
his statement
a note of how the tie
had come into her hands.
Tie?
It slid
at him from an envelope,
untwisting
like the skin off a shedding snake.

Inhalation, a cloyed spasm
to the drowned,
gave way to staring.
Slowly he turned away,
started writing—no,
drawing.
As though moving a wooden spoon
through batter,
he could only draw
the letters of the words,
letters which dipped and churned
and disappeared in semiliquid folds.
Circles, ovals,
loops
drawn in oozy air.
Phones and voices
down the hall,
shoes shuffling
toward him on the tiles,
the blind tube-light hum
of omniache,
thick stirring pen on paper,
all spiralled in
and down
and blurred.

V

DISEMBODIED in a sway of sky
he saw himself at home,
searching familiar stillness,
her presence loose in the air
like milk scent,
her things gathered up in boxes.
Transfigured in his mind,
she stood
among the altered, angled shadows
of belongings.
The back corners of his sight
kept being convinced
she had just stepped outside the room,
and then he came upon the knight.
Black,
almost glowing
purple with dark phosphorescence
and a sheen
like obsidian's refracted cleavage,
it tipped into his hand,
pulling with it bright links
of silver chain

ONDINA

which poured
into his palm
and pooled like mercury.

VI

Eyelids lifting open now,
his lashes catch a flickering light
cast on the house through branches.
Like a pack of wild children,
the shadow dogs come tearing
around the house; they romp and call,
flow in bounds beyond the hillcrest
and disappear down toward the river.
As he watches from the fringes
of transplant groves,
the sculpted, picked and pruned
garden malaise
they now call River Park,
he senses he has disappeared that way,
he and Karin
and the river and the knight.
How had she put it?
All the names
you call out in the night
begin with K.
    K—K1 (King to King One)
    N x N*ch* (Knight takes Knight: Check)

Carving monograms
across deep runic space
had pared away the awe,
the plainest, open face.

Her face—
it opens in the Dream.
The Old Man's face,
the mirrored face,
the gnarls of Billy Hitch's grace,
that hawk swooping through his dream,
the hawk-nosed beauty of her face,
all circle in the liquid sky of waking.

A bad fall, he hears.
You've been raving. The voice of O
is coming from his chest.
Now, look again, it says.
This is a picture of the house.

Who is this talking?
Now? he asks. *Who? Look now?*
His own voice fizzes with the gnats,
an effervescent sparkle in his head.

Doctor, I think he's coming around.

Around. Around. The whole thing's—
The whole thing's a-coming round.

Look at me, the woman says.
Who am I?

You are—me, he says. *No. Ondina.*
But you are gone.

No, you are you, she says,
and I'm not gone.
You can be you now.
You won't die now. You are you.

Yeah, you, he says. *I'm—*
and you are—

I'm Ondina.

Yes, he says. *The blonde.*
The woman in the robe.
The K inside the night.
You died. You died.

She shakes her head and laughs,
Blonde only in a flash of lightning.
I'm Ondina. I am dark.
I didn't die.
You almost died.

He remembers dying,
hanging in the cold,
swirling down. Something of him
surely died and swirled down.
Who died then?
Karin?
Died? And Kate?
They caromed off and K'ed? Or died?

Karin wasn't real, she says.
You've been raving.

Wasn't real?

Well, real enough
to get you started.
Your ravings were inspired,
but ravings all the same.

I saw you, he says.
Your eyes.
You hung them on a silver chain
and twisted in the night.

I'm here—Ondina,
flesh and bone.
Just stay awake.
We'll work it out.
Don't go back to sleep yet.

What is this mirror?
You're all I see.

You fell, she says.
It's not a mirror; it's a picture.
The doctors have shown you pictures.
That one's of me, not you.
And I am me.

I felt you in me.

So I see.

I fell? he asks.

You hit a tree, flew off a cutbank.
An old man found you hanging
by your pack strap
in a dead spruce snag.
You must have been skiing down awfully fast.

I got free.

You got wracked up,
punctured, almost killed.
You got pneumonia.
You've got fluid on your lungs.
You almost drowned.

I got free.
I was coming for you.

For me?
Or K?

For the one who sees
that, real or dreamed,
this whole thing
is for keeps.

Go back to sleep.

Wait.
You put this in my hand?
He holds out the knight and chain.

Thought it might help you make it.
From here on in, though,
take it just as a reminder.
The chain works by linking,
not by binding.
It's a different kind of free.
Knight takes Knight.
Fifty-Fifty.
Check?
Now rest.
You've come up from very deep.
Do you think that you can rest now?

The night closed in,
and he could dream real dreams again.
Cool wet cloths lay on his brow.
The river was alive.
He heard the Old Man's splashy laugh;
his voice spoke well of dreams:

> "Sometimes it takes a dream of death
> to live with the bitch that's rooted in you.
> It's wild, aint it?
> Some kill, and some get killed.
> But who's to say what's real or not,
> when dreams lay open spooky life,
> and life comes a-swirlin at you dreamin?"

Book Four

Flow of the Bright Dark

AND now he dreams the waking dream,
feels anew the cold droplet
on his nape,
the true shiver
of unbounded power.
The Female comes alive.
The undertow
flows on.
Twilight swells through day and night.
The moon flows out its inky white.
Conscious scribings
wash to nothing.
Stains are not an end.
The flow
keeps rolling,
washing stone,
whirling,
swelling
wave to wave,
a returning Being
in the night,
the Being that returns

to mold
the paper globule
of Hornet's nest
Time and Time again,
the nest that crumbles
in the hand,
but flowing
from the moistness
of mouth
and gut,
flows on,
expanding,
chambered egg by egg,
cell by cell,
the world chewed,
spat out,
shat and laid
and whirled
in variegated grays,
buff-blues,
black coils,
and oiled white larvae,
perfect,
waiting with their eyespot
and salmon-tail
urgings,
dark red as blood-waves
over shoals,
the gathering of days
spun
in the eyeball swirls
of planetary glue,
a growing sphere

of growing.

And in its heaves
of growth,
the cold mountain
sways
under the white-dark storm,
falls full under lustre,
flashing spruce-blue,
pushing the white clouds
up,
up through folds of violet,
booming silver billows
up to the black anvil.
And the dark wet flow
rolls down,
hallowing the ground
in the pounding
dark compounding
name of Thunder,
shatter-power, loose
across the land,
crackling white
exploding godheads on the hunt,
exploding rapid courses
down through boulders,
ripping, rending,
tearing open
Space
and the universe of Time.
Flash—
the ground quakes
in waves.

In the beginning,
there was Sound.

Rabbit,
Deer,
Coyote,
Ghost,
strike out of light-leap,
leave frozen auras
afloat
behind quicksilver bounds for cover.
Swallows plummet.
Gnats dissolve.
The Hawk catches a blast
of seared air,
veers
hard north,
blown with torn barbules
along the high keen edge
of country that can kill.
Lightning,
savage whitewater
of the storm,
rips the pounding river
of the sky.
Rain slashes down,
down the cold mountain.
Black crumbling cumulus
falls behind the mesa
and pours out across the plains.
And the torn Universe expands
around its wounds
and disappears

to—*Flash*—reappear
and wound again.
Burned bodies
take on shadow shapes,
leap down the slopes of space
as starlight,
falling down,
soaking back into the earth,
the dark spark of humus
sucked by roots.

And the flash opens
visions to him,
a man and woman
walking,
wading,
swimming
in the river,
flowing in the walking rain,
wet gleam of bodies
flashed in the peril
of crackling light,
then arms shining full
in shatters
of filtered sunlight,
sunlight curved round a shoulder,
sunlight lapped by water
and dissolved in waves around a thigh,
light transforming into shadow waves
even as it pierces mists aslant
through vapor clearings in the west,
laying lambence
on beads of water

rolling off a breast,
on heads thrown back in laughter,
on a work-scarred sun-browned hand
curving round
a belly
that is filling up with child,
on human beings full aswim
in being,
spirit-spirals
of the Wavy Mystery,
the earthly radiance,
wearing the naked
shadow power
of days and nights
around their necks,
swaying on bright droplet links
of silver chains.

Lightning vision seizes leaps,
but the animal flows on
through twilight after-flash.
Light and Darkness
make their Dance
in the serpent-birthing swirl
of Mother Rattlesnake.
Her newborn tangle of black ringlets
shines in wet curling
reflections of the sky
and sparkles
with a thousand bright round eyes.
Some feed Raven.
Some feed Hawk.
Some die away

to feed the grasses
and so turn into different swirls
in the belly of the Elk,
then to a leanly rippled
gift of haunch
pulled apart by teeth.
Some wend their way
to sun
and on,
empowered of the Silence
and the galactic turns of Snake,
spiralling
the secret Serpent Dance
of homage
to the majesty of caves.
Mother, the Earth of Gaia,
opens her skin,
emerging larger,
gliding smoothly
into darker coils
of gleaming Diamondback.
It is the fluid bidding
of the Universe
the Serpent offers back,
the truth of home,
the light-dark way
of seasons whirled in night snows,
held in melt pools,
passed between the moonlight
and the summer dawn
as dew,
and the eternal depths
of light and dark

beamed
off the black carapace
of an ant.

It is the fluid bidding
of the Snake
that shows the way,
the miracle
of primal motion
and the power held
in one clear droplet
from a fang.
Then she rolls
her long sliding hips
down
along the river-curves of spine,
swimming the earth,
sidewinding waves
of being
and away.

The rumbling sky
leaves its undulations
soaking in the ground.
The walking rain sweeps on;
and behind its distant booms,
circles of quiet
eddy back.
Leaves lie pummelled.
Green things try unbowing.
A split cottonwood
eases down a limb
on a peeled slab of trunk.

Birds test breath
and then with murmured calls
slowly relace the air.
The black river of the sky slides
downrange to feed
on swollen golden pollen cones
and peach-fold
billows
mounting across the plains.

The land lies still,
a huge beast
on its back,
stunned
and slowly afloat
in the flowing female
river of its soul,
the fluid power
of inhaled dark.
And he feels the flow
beneath him
move within.
The power given in a breath
flows Female through him,
in him,
in his own arising from the earth,
in the vapor rising,
and in the flowing fall of water
back to home.

The woman
takes a searing breath,
grunts deep.

Her waters break.
The last drop
upon his nape
opens the center
of all things,
the opening
of all the skies
of all his days and nights,
evolved beyond
the ways of disappearance.
First the pivot
of a man
is born,
and then the man.

He pulls another blade of grass
and with it draws her real
initial in the air,
tries to focus
it against the vapor waves
above the prairie's rivulating green.
The white tip rolls
the letter out,
simple script and lolling, O.
He sees the curves expand
and roll and drift far out
into another and another,
and they begin
and rebegin her name
and loop and circle
and refocus in late sun,
black-silver arced ellipses
zipped by gnats—

her eyes.

And the river bends
and bends him down
to cup one hand,
the other holding strong
with grass, fingers
clenched like roots
along the crumbling banks,
his curved palm
reaching down
to cup a drink.

The glide
comes into him
and slides
down with sacred waters
coming home
from sky to ground
to underground
and curving to the sea,
feeding
the wonder
and the woe
of roots,
tangled
in the living grass roots
reaching down,
tangled in the dead,
feeding,
growing
in the swells,
the swelling growing Now

of Time's expanding ocean,
always pregnant,
swollen
with the undercurrents of Future-Past,
of earthquakes,
the enduring promises of sharks' teeth
left on mountaintops,
of tidal swirls crossbedded
in the tilt
of desert sandstone,
of waves of thunder,
waves of leap,
Antelope
bounding down the mounds
of prairie, following the folds
of watercourse,
of ripples coming home,
all coming,
swaying through him,
all within him
as with Ondina,
first cell born,
first bearing cell,
the ancient holder
of the spiral
and dark youngling
of the Old.

    She'll come.
    She'll come.

The LightDark
roars apart the mælstrom

then slips away,
swirls
along the river bank,
rewhirls curves behind
the cold flicked-pebble kiss
as water closes over stone,
washing smooth
the grooves of scribes,
washing the Dark Old One,
washing the Companion
and the Dance,
washing through dreamed darkness
and the killer
and the song,
washing sunlight,
bright blue
day sky
held within the sheen
of waves,
washing stillness,
laughter's old white bone,
the bone sniffed out
among the grasses
and taken in the jaws
of old Grandfather Dog
who trots off with that dry white
honeycomb of cells
long washed and weathered clean
of marrow stains,
who trots off with that bone
in his mouth,
who gnaws it wet
and brings back the taste,

who takes it up
and heads on out,
who carries that old bone
off in his teeth
and lopes down
the pebbled bank,
loping easy,
washed in moonlight,
washed in twilight,
dawnlight,
daylight,
washed in night,
on downslope,
fluid loping down,
down the pebbled bank,
who splashes on into the dark and silver river,
into the spirit-glinting flow
that holds all reflections
of all the skies
of nights and days,
on into the black-bright waves,
swimming,
bearing undulations
into the wavy dark,
urging,
coming on,
on with the white bone,
surging fluid white
on home in the black
flash-bright
waves
the waves

of home
  come home
    of home
      come home.

Epilogue

The Walking Rain

THE clouds mount dark as wild plums
in sunlit willow baskets
on my shoulders
as I unfold and stand
and once again begin to walk
and dream my wild fruit dreams
out of the rooted earth.
I feel the slant sun touch
my face from clear across the world;
although, it is the walk
that warms my chest
and bobs black light
against my breast,
as if starlight gleamed
from holly-grapes,
suspending dayshadow's purple
amulet of night
on a silver moonstruck stem.

The black fecund rolls of clouds
swell and start to overflow
and I lean on out,

pour down the mountain
and take up the rising stride
across the plains.
I walk loose
as streaks of water
curving down
and smell the rain's cold breath
come back into me in swelling silence.

The wet vital spark
ignites,
lights the cloud bones' veiny fruit
and shudders its booming breath
of thunder through me,
folds back
into the black billows,
booms
and streaks down again as rain,
falling oblique, the supple
sweeping footfall of a paw,
fluid slipping through great distance
down
as liquid purple shadows
soak underground
to recharge the deep cool cave lakes,
the secret holds
of Old.

Ahead, the old secret rises
in another breath,
first far away
then full and deep.
And as I swing into full stride,

I feel it remake my face
in wind and rain
and see the linked droplets
flash blood-red
to purple, falling,
searing white, vapor
rising, falling,
something lustrous black
still coming falling coming
across the wet flickering land of grasses,
on through blue-black light,
aurora green-black flickers, light
through rolling shadows,
wild, black-bright and secret,
and on down
the tangled filamentous pathways
to the white-dark roots,
the white
dark
whole
grace-entangled animal
of Soul.

The book was set Linotype by Bob Pounders in 12 pt. Garamond with hand-set display in Goudy Old Style composed by Tom Egan. Final composing was seen to by Robert DeVarenne and Lou Nolin and the edition printed letterpress by Paul Tabares at The Egan Printing Company, Denver.

The book was designed by Lanie Kohler. The illustrations were engraved for letterpress from drawings by Jake Pinello. The text paper is alkaline Olde White from Howard. The edition was Smyth sewn by Hawley of Denver, 800 copies bound in Curtis Flannel and 200 copies bound in cloth over boards which have been numbered and signed by the poet and artist.